Grasslands
Around the World

Grasslands Around the World

by Corinne J. Naden

illustrated with photographs and maps

Franklin Watts, Inc.
575 Lexington Avenue
New York, N.Y. 10022

←A FIRST BOOK→

For Tess and Zito Carbone

Also by the author
THE FIRST BOOK OF RIVERS

Photographs courtesy of:

Charles Phelps Cushing: opp. page 1, pages 30, 59 (S.C.S. from Cushing)
New York Public Library Picture Collection: title page, pages 2, 3, 4, 8, 15, 24, 27, 33, 37, 38, 39, 44, 46, 49, 53
Sawders-Cushing: pages 19, 23, 42, 54
United Press International: pages 13, 26, 56, 58
U. S. Department of Agriculture: page 18

Cover photo (courtesy Sawders from Cushing) shows a farm on the Canadian prairie.

MAPS BY GEORGE BUCTEL

SBN 531-00714-6

Copyright © 1970 by Franklin Watts, Inc.
Library of Congress Catalog Card Number: 72-117184
Printed in the United States of America

2 3 4 5

Contents

Grasslands are the world's best places to grow food.

What Are Grasslands?

Perhaps you have seen a picture of tall grasses blowing gently in the wind. Or perhaps you have actually stood in the middle of a prairie, where grasses taller than a grown person stretched as far as you could see. Then you know that a tallgrass prairie is one of the prettiest sights in nature.

The tallgrass prairies are pleasing to see, but they are becoming difficult to find. Much of the prairie has been plowed under for planting crops. But long ago, this natural prairie covered about one-third of the land that became the United States.

Prairies are very important to you and to everyone. They are important because they are grasslands — the world's best places to grow food. A *grassland* is an area that has a natural cover of grass instead of trees. And grass is the most important of all plants to man.

Why is grass such an important plant? If you stop to think for a moment, you can probably come up with many reasons. The biggest reason is food.

Over 4 billion people live on some 50 million square miles of the earth's surface. The rest of the earth — almost 75 percent — is covered by water. People must feed themselves, and all other creatures must eat, too. But getting enough food becomes a problem as the population of the world increases and farmland is plowed under to make room for the growing number of people.

Grasses are the largest of all the plant families. They cover about one-fifth of the land area on earth. Although there are about seven thousand different kinds of grasses, man and grazing animals mainly eat grass plants from three large groups. They are pasture grasses, cereals, and sweet grasses.

Sugarcane in Hawaii

Pasture grasses, such as bluegrass, buffalo grass, and Bermuda grass, grow on plains and prairies. They are good grazing food for cattle. In the winter the cattle eat the dried grass, which has become hay.

Cereal grasses are probably the most familiar to you. They are grains which have seeds that can be eaten, such as rice, oats, wheat, corn, barley, millet, and rye.

Sweet grasses are so called because their juices are sweet. These grasses are used to make sugar and molasses. The most important sweet grass is sugarcane.

Have you thought of any reasons besides food that make grasses important? For one thing, they are pleasant to look at. A rich green lawn or a cool, inviting park may be as pleasing to the eye as a great prairie. Grasses also make the soil richer and they help to prevent floods. Soil that has no grasses growing on it is easily washed away by water, or it may become dry and blow away in the wind. Grasses give us products that we use every day. *Bamboos*, a large group of tall, fast-growing grasses, are used to make furniture, paper, and other items. This grass grows in Central and South America, and in the Orient. Some bamboo is also grown in the United States.

In different parts of the world, grasslands may be called by different names. But they are all somewhat alike. You have probably heard each of these grassland names before.

"Lea" (lee), "meadow," and "pasture" are all words that mean a grassy place to graze animals. A lea may also be used to grow hay. Since a meadow is often near water, the land may be moist.

Bamboo growing near Savannah, Georgia

Animals need rich pastureland.

A *plain* is a large and mostly level area of land. It has few, if any, trees and is covered by shortgrasses. Plains are usually found at low elevations and have a semidry climate. (This area in the United States is called the *Great Plains*; in the USSR it is the *steppe*; and in Argentina it is known as the *pampa*.)

Prairies are treeless areas covered by tall natural grasses.

A *savanna* is a level, treeless plain in a warm climate.

The *tundra* is the level, treeless plain of the Arctic.

A *veld* is a grassland in Africa.

4

Where Are Grasslands?

Just like the tallgrass prairie, there are not many grassland areas that can be seen today in their natural state. Man has made many changes on them. But whatever their condition, grasslands can be found in most parts of the world. (See the map on pages 6 and 7.)

Grasslands cover large parts of mid-North America and South America. They are found in central and southern Africa, in the form of velds and savannas. (Some small savanna lands are also found in the southeastern United States.) Northern Europe and Asia (the steppes) and parts of northern and eastern Australia are grasslands.

Each of these grasslands helps to feed the people of the world.

Grasslands in the United States

Before the United States became a country, even before Columbus discovered the New World, great stretches of forests and acre upon acre of grasslands covered the North American continent. In fact, about half of what later became the United States was once forested areas, or woodlands. About one-third of it was grasslands, and about one-sixth was desert.

The original grasslands stretched mainly in a huge triangle from Canada nearly to Mexico. The point of the triangle reached into what is now the state of Illinois, and the base sat against the Rocky Mountains in the West. This entire area was a place of few trees, level land, and thick grasses.

ARCTIC OCEAN

NORTH
AMERICA

ATLANTIC

PACIFIC

OCEAN

SOUTH
AMERICA

OCEAN

Grasslands

ARCTIC OCEAN

EUROPE

ASIA

PACIFIC

OCEAN

AFRICA

INDIAN   OCEAN

MADAGASCAR

AUSTRALIA

NEW ZEALAND

GRASSLANDS OF THE WORLD

There were also patches of grasslands in other parts of the country. The Central Valley of California is a great, fertile plain, and eastern Washington and Oregon were once large, natural grasslands. Smaller areas — the savannas — were found in the warmer southeastern United States.

There are still some natural grasslands left, but most of them have changed. As man began to settle in the New World, he needed land for crops, for homes, and for towns. Much of the land was plowed to raise crops to feed a growing nation.

Today there are two major grassland areas in the United States. They are called the Great, or High, Plains and the prairie.

The flat, treeless plains of North Dakota

The Great Plains

What do you see when you think of the Great Plains? Do you see mighty Indian tribes hunting the wandering bison herds? Perhaps you think of brave explorers sailing their canoes through the winding turns of the Missouri River. Or perhaps you have heard of the range wars fought between men who made their living from raising cattle and those who raised sheep.

All those pictures — and more — were once true about the Great Plains. And even though the Indians and the bison herds are mostly gone, even though explorers no longer chart the muddy Missouri in canoes, the Great Plains is still a special place.

The United States covers 3,022,387 square miles, not counting Alaska and Hawaii. The Great Plains cover 586,461 square miles, or about one-fifth of the country. They stretch from the foothills of the Rockies to western Texas, Oklahoma, Kansas, Nebraska, and the Dakotas. Four other states are also part of the Great Plains; eastern New Mexico, Colorado, Wyoming, and Montana, making ten Plains states in all. The Great Plains are 750 miles wide at their widest point and are 1,600 miles long.

The climate of the Great Plains is called semiarid, which means "half dry." But that does not mean that the Great Plains are dry half of the time and wet the other half. It means that in some years a lot of rain falls on the Great Plains. In other years, rain is scarce. When it does rain, it falls mostly from May through July and averages about twenty inches or less a year. (The average rainfall in arid — dry — lands is below ten to fifteen inches a year. In humid — wet — areas, rainfall is about thirty to fifty inches.)

Most plains are less than 500 feet above sea level. But the Great Plains average over 1,500 feet. That is why they are also called the

GREAT PLAINS OF THE UNITED STATES

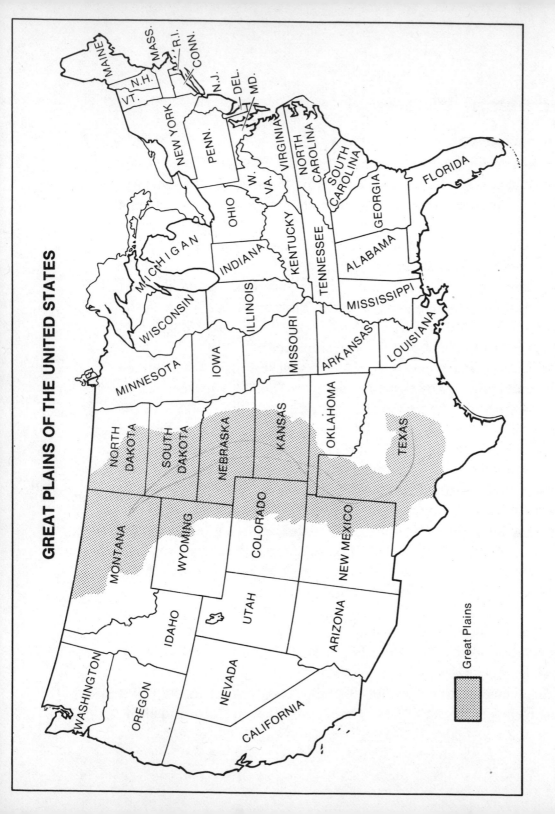

Great Plains

High Plains. The Plains are higher in the west, near the Rocky Mountains, than they are in the east. This is because the land in the eastern section has been so worn down by rivers and streams.

The soil of the Great Plains is very dark in color and it contains alkaline salt. This salt sometimes rises to the surface and stunts or kills plants. However, the soil of the Great Plains is among the most fertile in the world. It would be even more so if the rainfall were dependable.

As you know, plains are usually flat. The Great Plains have no high mountains, and they also do not have large bodies of water. This lack of mountains and huge lakes has a great deal to do with the rainfall.

In order for rain to fall, two masses of air must bump into each other. Mountains and large bodies of water direct, or steer, air masses. But the air masses that flow over the Great Plains have nothing to steer them. And so they flow about the region in an undirected way. If two of them bump, there is rain. If they do not bump, there is no rain. So, the climate is unpredictable. There may be a drought one season and a flood the next. Warm weather and good rain may bring a fine, early growing season. But the crops may be killed the next month by a late spring frost. Weather is hard to figure out in the Great Plains.

The people on the Plains have had to learn to live with the changeable weather. They have had to learn to live with periods of little rain or long droughts. And that is also true of the plants and animals that make their homes on the Plains.

The first thing you would probably notice if you took a tour of the Great Plains is that there are very few trees. As you know, a lack of trees is common to plains areas. The natural cover of the Plains is shortgrass, and, in fact, the region is sometimes called "shortgrass country." These grasses are able to live well in the climate of the Plains. During a drought some can quickly draw in what little mois-

11

ture there is on the surface of the land. Some push their roots to the surface when there is no water deeper in the soil.

There are many shortgrasses found over the Great Plains. These are some of the most important:

Buffalo grass, in the central and southern Plains. This short-grass grows close together, five to eight inches high. Nearly all livestock like it. It can survive long periods of heavy grazing better than any other native grass.

Blue grama grass can live in sandier soil than can buffalo grass, and it covers a large part of the Plains. It grows about twelve to eighteen inches high.

Side oats grama is found over most of the Plains, except in northern Montana, North Dakota, and southern Texas. It has deep roots, which help it to survive a drought, and it is very hardy.

Western wheatgrass grows in the northern and central Plains, and in some parts of the south. At harvesttime it looks very much like a field of wheat.

Many years ago large herds of bison roamed over the Great Plains. Perhaps no other animal was so well suited to this region. These huge dark beasts traveled the Plains in search of food and water. Bison can stand very hot or very cold temperatures. They have great strength and endurance. They can live a long time on little food and water. During a storm, bison will stop and face into the wind. Cattle will keep moving. Therefore, unlike cattle, bison are not apt to fall over a cliff or into a snow-covered ravine during a storm.

The wandering bison herds were very important to the Indians of the Great Plains. Bison meat provided food, the skin was used for clothing and shelter, and tools were made from the bones.

Left, a buffalo herd on the Great Plains; right, grasshoppers take over a field of hay.

During the early nineteenth century, the white man realized that the bison's meat and hide were very valuable. White hunters began to kill the huge animals by the thousands. By 1900 these senseless killings accounted for 50 million Plains bison. The animals were almost extinct.

The American Bison Society was formed in 1905 to end the slaughter of the Plains bison. It did manage to save a few herds. Today there are over 30,000 bison in the United States and Canada.

The pronghorn antelope is another animal that has become a rare sight on the Great Plains. The pronghorn stands about three feet tall at the shoulders, and it can run at a speed of over 60 miles an hour. It has good eyesight and hearing, and it lives entirely on the vegetation of the Plains.

The Great Plains are filled with all kinds of wildlife. Prairie dogs, for instance, live in colonies, with perhaps several hundred of them to one prairie dog town. The prairie dog is not a dog at all but a kind of squirrel. It is well suited to the Plains because it is able to produce its own moisture inside its body.

Jackrabbits live on the Plains in great numbers. They have good hearing, speed, and sight. The adult jackrabbit is usually buff-colored, or sometimes darker. But in winter it turns nearly all white and is very hard to see in the snow.

An enemy of both the prairie dog and the jackrabbit is the coyote. It also eats rodents and dead and young animals. The coyote is a good hunter with great speed.

The grasshopper is not an animal, but this insect has often made life miserable for those who live on the Plains. Grasshoppers are sensitive to changes in the weather, and weather changes can happen often on the Plains. When grasshoppers sense a change in the weather and begin to move, their great hordes may blot out the sun. In their frenzy, they will even attack wooden fences or posts.

The white man has lived on the Great Plains since the Spanish founded Santa Fe, New Mexico, in 1609. (Jamestown, Virginia, England's first permanent settlement in the New World, was founded only two years earlier.)

The Spanish explored and began to settle in some parts of the Great Plains. They wanted English settlers to live there, too. So, they offered eight hundred acres of land for only forty dollars. But not many people came, perhaps because Spain said that the new settler had to become a Catholic and a Spanish citizen, too.

After the American Revolution (1775–83), the young United States began to push westward. The Santa Fe Trail was opened in the early nineteenth century. Traders, settlers, gold seekers, and adventurers began to brave about eight hundred dangerous miles between Independence, Missouri, and Santa Fe, New Mexico. But people still did not settle the Plains in any great numbers. The climate was severe

Indians on the plains

and the danger of Indian attack was very real. The Spanish were especially discouraged because they could not find gold in the area. Therefore, Spain secretly sold its territory to France around 1800.

The United States government learned about the "secret sale" in 1801. President Thomas Jefferson was very distressed. He did not want the land to be sold to any country but America. Finally, after long talks with France, the United States bought the so-called Louisiana Territory on May 2, 1803, for $15,000,000. That gave the young country 825,000 additional square miles of land. Included were what would become the states of North and South Dakota, Montana, Wyoming, Colorado, Missouri, Arkansas, and Louisiana. A large part of that territory was the Great Plains.

Even though there was a good deal of exploration in the West after the Louisiana Purchase, the Plains still did not invite many settlers. Part of the reason may have been due to Major Stephen H. Long (1784–1864), an American army officer.

15

Major Long headed an expedition to the Yellowstone region in 1819–20. His journey took him to what would become the states of Wyoming, Idaho, and Montana. The major's expedition was pretty much of a failure. However, he did make a map of his trip. On the map he labeled the Great Plains as "the Great American Desert." That was how people came to think of the region. For a long time no one seemed very anxious to settle there. Instead, the Plains became a sort of corridor to get from east to west.

Those who did settle on the Plains had to fight the weather and the Indians. The Plains Indians were the most warring of the Indian tribes in the New World. They included the Comanches, the best horsemen; the Blackfoot; the Crow; the Cheyenne; the Apache; and the Arapaho.

As we know, the Indians of the Plains depended upon the bison for survival. They lived a life of hunting and following the bison herds. But when the white man came, the Indian was doomed. When the bison herds were killed off, he lost his way of life. After wandering the Plains freely, the Indian found it difficult or impossible to adapt to life on a reservation, to which the white man sent him. The Indian fought desperately, but he could not win. In 1876 the Sioux, under Sitting Bull, defeated General George Custer at the Battle of Little Bighorn. That was the Indians' last great stand.

After the Civil War (1861–65), people began to enter the Great Plains in increasing numbers. The first permanent settlers were the cattlemen. At first, they had gone there to feed and supply the wagon trains going west. But they found that the stretches of level land and shortgrasses were well suited to cattle. And so they stayed.

The cattlemen were a hardy breed. And they had to be. The winters of 1885–86 and 1886–87 brought such terrible blizzards that the cattle industry was almost wiped out. From 40 to 90 percent of the herds were lost.

Then the sheep herds trekked up from the Southwest. Sheep needed less grass and water than cattle, and the Great Plains was an ideal place for them, too. Not surprisingly, trouble brewed into range wars between sheepherder and cattleman over rights to the rich grazing lands. But the sheepherders were also hardy men, and they stayed on the Plains, too.

During the late nineteenth and early twentieth centuries, people who wanted good farmland began to move onto the Plains. The Homestead Act had been passed in 1862. It said that anyone who was a citizen and either the head of a family or twenty-one years old could have up to 160 acres of land. After five years of living on the land or cultivating it — and not leaving it for more than a six-month period — the settler could own the land if he paid certain fees. Or he could buy his land after six months; the price was about $1.25 an acre.

Now the population began to increase rapidly on the Great Plains. For instance, Kansas gained half a million people in a seven-year period. The farmers, too, were hardy men. And like the ranchers, they also had to be. In the mid-1870's they suffered four years of destruction by grasshoppers. In 1888 came the great blizzard. The next year brought dust storms; and floods came two years later. In 1889–90 a long drought caused much hardship.

But the settler on the Great Plains also brought much hardship upon himself. Cattlemen were careless with their grazing lands. They allowed their herds to graze the same lands all year long. The Indians had moved their herds about, giving the grass time to grow. The sheepherders allowed their sheep to chew the grass to the roots. In this dry region, where grass grows slowly, many acres of grazing land were destroyed. The grass was eaten to the roots and died. Bare patches of land grew larger and larger.

The farmer was careless, too. He had come to the Plains from the moist eastern lands, and he began to farm the Plains in the ways of

17

the East. Year after year he planted the same crops until the land was worn out. He did not realize that in this semidry region, the land was easily robbed of its minerals. In periods of no rain, the winds carried away the dry topsoil. When the rains came, they made deep gullies in the worn-out soil.

It was these bad farming and grazing practices, plus the long droughts of 1934–37, that gave a new name to the Great Plains. They were now called "the Dust Bowl." (John Steinbeck wrote his famous novel *The Grapes of Wrath* about this period and the terrible hardships it caused.) These years of drought caused many people to leave the Plains.

The people who stayed had to learn new farming and grazing practices. Cattlemen moved their herds from pasture to pasture, giving the grass time to grow. Farmers planted crops that would return minerals to the soil. They no longer planted the same crops in the same soil year after year. They irrigated their fields and planted some overgrazed fields with grass.

Today, the Great Plains remain a prized agricultural area. This huge and fertile grassland produces livestock, grains, cotton, and vegetables to feed a hungry and growing world.

Abandoned farm in Oklahoma during the Dust Bowl years

The Prairie

The tallgrass prairie is a beautiful place. At one time it stretched from Ohio to eastern Oklahoma, Kansas, Nebraska, and the Dakotas, where it joined the Great Plains. It also included parts of Minnesota, Wisconsin, Indiana, Illinois, Iowa, Missouri, and Texas. Today the natural tallgrass prairie is almost gone. But you can still see some of it in places such as southern and east-central Kansas, along the western border of Iowa, in the national forest near Halsey, Nebraska, and in refuges in North and South Dakota and other prairie states as well.

Some scientists say that there is no real difference between the prairie and the plains. Others say that the huge grassland in the middle of the United States can be divided into three regions: the shortgrass prairie (the Great Plains), the mixed-grass prairie (where plains and prairie meet), and the tallgrass prairie.

Rain on the prairie

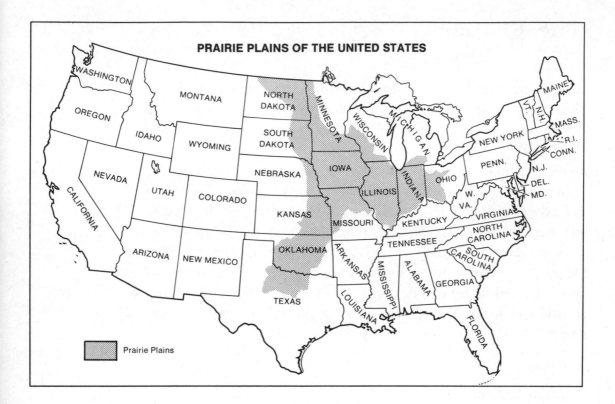

PRAIRIE PLAINS OF THE UNITED STATES

Prairie Plains

Because the prairie covers such a large part of the country, the climate varies a great deal, depending upon where you are. Autumn comes to Minnesota before it makes its way to Oklahoma. The first buds of spring blossom earlier in Texas than in Wisconsin. In the eastern part of the prairie, the climate is a lot like that of the forested areas in the eastern United States. However, the winters are colder and the summers are warmer on the prairie. Farther west the prairie climate becomes more like that of the Great Plains, with less and less rainfall. Overall, the prairie averages about thirty inches of rain a year (as compared to about twenty inches for the Great Plains).

Like the Great Plains, the prairie is called treeless. But in the case of the prairie that is not really true. The many streams in the prairie states are lined with trees, and there are forests in the narrow valleys through which the streams flow. Bur oak, cottonwood, willow, elm, and red cedar trees are there. But most of the prairie's natural cover is grass.

At one time thousands of miles of prairie were covered by *big bluestem*, the most common of the prairie grasses. Growing as high as six feet, it is still an important pasture grass in Oklahoma, Kansas, and Nebraska. Big bluestem is also called turkeyfoot because the top of the stalk branches out like the foot of a turkey. But so much good prairie soil has been plowed under that big bluestem may be extinct within fifty years.

Little bluestem, also called prairie beardgrass, grows in much the same areas as big bluestem. Livestock like this grass, which usually does not grow over four feet high.

Indian grass is found in the western prairie. It is tall — four to six feet — and has brown or copper seed heads. Other prairie grasses include *switch grass*, a tall, bunchy plant, and *needlegrasses*, with long slender stems.

About one hundred and fifty different kinds of natural grasses grow on the prairie. Where the rainfall is good, the grasses completely cover the ground. Where the rainfall is scarce, the grasses may be clumped together in bunches. These grasses give livestock good pastureland and plenty of hay.

Crowded in among the prairie grasses are lovely flowering plants.

They bring color and beauty to the prairie lands. Sunflowers and goldenrods bloom in autumn, and roses in the spring. Coneflowers with gay yellow heads dot the prairie; so do delicate-looking prickly-pear blossoms. The open prairie also has many shrubs, such as the silvery leadplant which grows among the bluestem grasses, and choke-cherry, wild plum, and the bright orange butterfly weed.

Many different kinds of animals share the plant life of the prairie. In earlier times great herds of bison roamed there, as well as on the Great Plains. The mule deer likes the brushy parts of the prairie. This large-eared animal was once hunted almost to extinction. Now it is slowly increasing in numbers. It lives around rivers and streams.

Many, many small animals live on and under the prairie soil. White-footed mice are found practically everywhere. A great number of them are eaten by animals, birds, and snakes. But the mice reproduce very quickly, and so they have not become extinct.

Besides mice, the prairie is home to gophers and weasels, foxes and moles. The badger is a rare sight today, although sometimes you may catch a glimpse of this animal as it hisses and snarls its way into its burrow. The kangaroo rat lives in the western prairie. It seldom needs anything to drink and can live for three months without water. Raccoons, skunks, and minks are fairly common sights on prairie lands.

Birds and insects add to the many kinds of life on the prairie. Great blue herons make their nests in cottonwood trees, and meadowlarks sound their pleasant whistle almost everywhere. There are curlews, owls, plovers, magpies, sandpipers, and geese. The prairie chicken used to live in the eastern and central prairie, but it is now found farther west. The male bird is a very dramatic performer. In the early morning and late evening the prairie chicken males gather together and go through complicated dances. A male will select a spot on the ground and spread its tail. Then it makes great "booming" noises by inflating the bright orange sacs on each side of its neck. Sometimes

Mule deer

the birds get into fights during the dances, and there is a great deal of hopping into the air and beating of wings. But usually not much harm is done to any of the birds.

Prairie birds include insects in their diet. Prairie insects live on the flowers and plants of the land. Besides the grasshopper, there are beetles, crickets, butterflies, bees, and ants. Harvester ants build cone-shaped homes from six to twelve inches high and from three to five feet at the base. The seeds that they pick up from the prairie are stored in special chambers by the ants. They also collect dead insects.

The prairie is about 300 to 1,400 feet above sea level. The soil is very rich and deep. That is a large part of the reason why so much natural grass covering has been plowed under for agriculture. Prairie soil is dark in color. It is made up of fine pieces that make the land very hard when it has dried after a wetting.

The great prairie grasslands are now great farmlands. This fertile region supplies food for people all over the world.

The prairie was first settled largely because of livestock. When the Dutch founded New Amsterdam (later New York) in 1625, they

Sowing wheat on the prairie in the nineteenth century

brought cattle with them. By the next century, cattle were thriving all along the eastern coast. As more people came to America, more land was needed. The cattlemen first moved the herds to less thickly forested areas, and then finally to the prairie lands.

The farmer who began to settle on the prairie had a lot of the same troubles as did the homesteader on the Great Plains — harsh weather, drought, insects, fire. The prairie farmers were sometimes called sodbusters. They soon discovered that dirt and sod would cling to their wooden plows when they tried to clear the acres of tall grass. Of course, this made plowing a very hard and slow task. But the problem was solved in 1837 when John Deere invented the steel plow. And so the natural prairie began to disappear under the plow blade.

The prairie states today are all important agricultural lands.

Illinois was once nearly all tallgrass prairie. Today it is one of the top farm states in the country, mostly because of its rich black prairie soil. Illinois became the twenty-first state in 1818. It was named for the Illiniwek Indians, but one of its nicknames is Prairie State. Large numbers of farm people came to Illinois in the early nineteenth century. Today over four-fifths of the state is farmland. It leads the country in producing soybeans and is second in corn. It also grows wheat, oats, hay, rye, barley, vegetable crops, and livestock.

Indiana, the nineteenth state (admitted in 1816), ranks third in corn output. The state, whose name means "land of the Indians," is now heavily industrialized, but it is also rich in livestock and soybeans. The most fertile and productive soil is in the central region.

Iowa is a top farm state, too, and like Illinois was once nearly all tallgrass — mostly bluestem — prairie. The name is an Indian word that is said to mean "beautiful land." Iowa became the twenty-ninth state in 1846. Today 95 percent of it is farmland. It is number one in growing corn, but it also grows oats, soybeans, and other grains, as well as livestock, on its deep rich soil.

Eastern *Kansas* used to be tallgrass prairie land. The state's name comes from the Kansa tribe of Siouan Indians. In 1861 Kansas became the thirty-fourth state. It is mainly known as a wheat region, but it is also rich in corn and livestock.

Natural prairie grasses once covered western and southern *Minnesota*. The state's name comes from two Dakota Indian words — *minne*, meaning "water," and *sota*, which has many meanings, among them "the peculiar appearance of the sky on certain days." Therefore, the name is said to mean "sky-tinted water." Minnesota became the thirty-second state in 1858. It is the fifth most important farm state in the country, after California, Iowa, Illinois, and Texas. Three-fourths of its land is covered by farms and pastures, and it is rich in corn, hay, and dairy goods.

25

Growing wheat on the prairie

Missouri was made the twenty-fourth state in 1821. At that time tallgrass prairie covered much of the northwestern part. Its Indian name means "town of the big canoes." Today Missouri is best known for the livestock industry. It also grows corn, wheat, cotton, and tobacco.

Eastern and northern *Nebraska* was tallgrass prairie land when it became the thirty-seventh state in 1867. *Nebraska*, an Oto Indian word, means "flat water." Nebraska's rich soil produces corn, oats, wheat, alfalfa, rye, and barley.

Eastern *North Dakota* is prairie land. It became the thirty-ninth state in 1889. *Dakota* is a Sioux Indian word meaning "allies." The state's farms are large, and it is the number one producer of barley, number two in wheat and flaxseed, and it also grows rye and potatoes.

Ohio, admitted as the seventeenth state in 1803, has rolling plains in the western region. Its name comes from an Indian word that probably meant "great river." Although ranking high in industry, Ohio produces dairy products, wheat, soybeans, and corn.

The word *Oklahoma* is from two Choctaw Indian words — *okla* means "people" and *humma* means "red." Tallgrass prairie once covered some northern and eastern parts of the state. Oklahoma became the forty-sixth state in 1907. Cattle is the most important product, but it also grows wheat, cotton, corn, hay, and other crops.

Early cattle trails across the prairie and plains

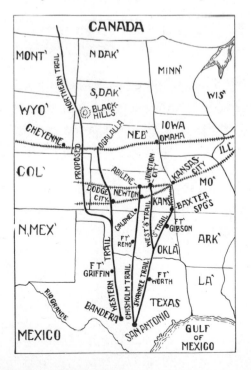

Eastern *South Dakota* is prairie region. It became the fortieth state in 1889, and it grows wheat, corn, oats, barley, hay, and livestock.

Texas has prairie land in the northeast. It became the twenty-eighth state in 1845. The name comes from an Indian word — *tejas* — meaning "friends." The soil of Texas is very good for raising livestock. Although it does produce many agricultural crops, it is highly important for its beef cattle, sheep, and wool production.

Prairie land in *Wisconsin* runs along the southwestern border of the state. Its Indian name is said to mean "gathering of the waters." Known as America's dairyland, Wisconsin became the thirtieth state in 1848. The northern part of the state is not good for farming, but Wisconsin grows cranberries, potatoes, vegetables, and grains, as well as dairy products.

Some Grasslands Around the World

They are called the steppe in the USSR, the pampa in Argentina, or the veld in Africa. They are all grasslands, almost level and nearly treeless. Like the Great Plains and the prairie in the United States, they are very important agricultural areas. They are the fertile plains which feed and clothe the world's people.

To see what grasslands are like around the world, let's visit five of them: the African veld, the Argentine pampa, the Australian lowlands, the Russian steppe, and that strange "grassland" known as the tundra.

The African Veld

Much of central and southern Africa is grassland, called savannas, or velds. Kenya, for instance, has savanna areas of thorn scrubs, with some scattered trees on the higher plains. The Republic of Ghana has grasslands along its coast, which broaden into the Accra plains. The Congo and Nigeria have savanna areas, as do all the African countries that occupy the east-central and southern regions of Africa.

Let us take a closer look at one of these African grasslands, the veld in South Africa.

Located at the tip of the African continent, the Republic of South Africa can boast of a wide change of scenery throughout its over 470,000 square miles. Most of the country is a great interior plateau, from 3,000 to 6,000 feet above sea level. This is the productive grassland known as the veld.

The veld can be divided into three major regions, plus a narrow strip — 3 to 30 miles wide — on the coast. The three major regions are: the Highveld, the Transvaal, and the Cape Middleveld.

The Highveld, also called the Northern Karoo, includes the Orange

Animals on the veld

Free State and some of the Cape of Good Hope Province. This very level plain is the country's most important grassland area. It produces 60 percent of the maize crop, 30 percent of the wheat, and most of the corn, beans, and potatoes. It is also a meat and dairy products region and is rich in minerals. (South Africa has an impressive supply of gold, uranium, and diamonds.) The Highveld is mostly above 4,000 feet, and its very even surface is broken by a few low ranges. (In South Africa, the flat-topped hills that are produced by erosion of a plateau are called *kopjes*.) Summers are warm and somewhat rainy, winters cool and dry. There is actually little rainfall on the Highveld,

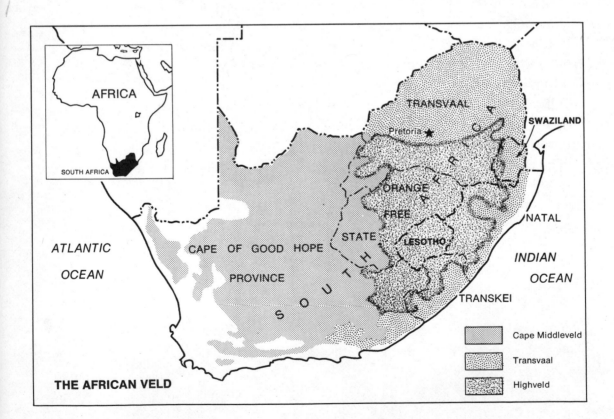

THE AFRICAN VELD

although thundershowers often do much damage and a drought may be followed by a downpour.

The Transvaal plateau basin is really a continuation of the Highveld. The capital city of Pretoria is in this region. The Transvaal is not as high as the Highveld and its climate is warmer. In summer the temperature rises above 80 degrees on most days. The rainfall is normally below thirty inches.

The Cape Middleveld, which merges at its northern part with the Highveld, is a smooth, dry area between 2,000 and 4,000 feet above sea level. It is located in the Cape of Good Hope Province and is also divided into the Southern or Little Karoo and the Central or Great Karoo. The rainfall in this region is heavier along the coast, where it is rare to have below-freezing temperatures.

The area of the Great Karoo is pastureland, used to graze thousands of sheep. The Highveld, in its native state, is typical grassland country and excellent farmland. North of the Highveld is wooded savanna. Scrub forests grow along the coast, known as the bush, or lowveld. Much of the South African land has been badly eroded, and, in the typical way of the plains, there are few forests.

Many of South Africa's animals live in its game reserves and national parks. Kruger National Park, some 8,000 square miles in the lowveld area, is the most famous. It is here that the cheetah, lion, leopard, elephant, and other native — but disappearing — South African animals may be seen. The country also has antelopes, buffaloes, rhinoceroses, and the springbok, a gazelle and the country's national emblem. South Africa also has many different kinds of birds and a good variety of fish, despite a lack of fresh water.

South Africa's soil allows the production of a great many agricultural crops, as well as all kinds of fruits. Much of its land is given to raising sheep, for the country is one of the world's leading producers of wool. Beneath the soil is a wealth of mineral treasures. But the crop yield of the South African farmer suffers greatly from soil erosion. Much of the fertile land has been, or is being, worn down by flash floods and water runoff. The low rainfall in other parts of the country makes those areas largely unusable for agriculture.

Agriculture has always been important to South Africa, as it is to much of Africa. The Dutch settled in the area in 1652. They did not intend to found a colony, but wanted a stopping-off point for the ships of the Dutch East India Company.

The British took over Cape Province in 1815, after the Napoleonic Wars, and began to bring English settlers into the area. But the tough and independent Dutch farmers — called Boers — opposed British settlement. The Boers set out across the land to found their own territory. They established two Boer republics — the Orange Free State and the Transvaal. But friction between the two peoples finally resulted in the South African, or Boer, War of 1899. After the British victory in 1902, the Union of South Africa came into being, composed of the British and Boer territories.

The union of British and Boer lands had been the dream of Cecil Rhodes (1853–1902), who had come to South Africa after diamonds were discovered in 1869. Rhodes eventually gained control of the country's diamond mines and also became the prime minister of the British cape colony.

South Africa sided with the Allies in both world wars and was severely hurt by the depression of the 1930's. But in 1948 its way of life underwent an even more drastic change. In that year Dr. Daniel Malan, of the National party, came into power, and the country began its still-existing policy of *apartheid* — racial separation. All succeeding prime ministers have upheld and strengthened that policy, despite protests by the United Nations, the British Commonwealth, and individual countries.

Apartheid means a life of almost complete separation between whites and nonwhites. There are different school systems, different churches, and different rules governing land ownership, jobs, voting rights, and almost any other aspect of life.

The Argentine Pampa

The Argentine Republic covers more than one million square miles. It is the second largest country in South America, the fourth largest in the Western Hemisphere, and the eighth largest in the world. The heart of this triangular-shaped nation is a fertile plain known as the pampa. The name comes from an Indian word meaning, appropriately enough, "flat area."

A cattle range on the pampa

The Argentine pampa forms a sort of semicircle from the Colorado River in the southeast to the Andes Mountains in the west, and north to the Chaco, or plantation regions. Its eastern boundary is the Atlantic Ocean. The semicircle has a radius of about 500 miles. Inside the semicircle is grown 95 percent of all the grain raised in this agricultural country. The pampa is Argentina's most valuable resource.

Because Argentina is in the Southern Hemisphere, summer comes to the pampa in January and winter in July. The country has a temperate climate, with hot summers in the northwest and cooler ones on the east coast. The rainfall is sometimes heavy — about forty inches a year in the northwest and thirty-seven inches around Buenos Aires, the capital. But parts of the pampa do go through periods of drought.

Sometimes warm air from the north collides with cool winds from the south. They produce violent storms over the Buenos Aires region. Strong winds, called *pamperos*, often sweep across the plains. But, in general, the pampa boasts mild temperatures and fairly regular rainfall. Those are two important reasons why it is one of the world's best farming regions.

The pampa is naturally covered with typical grasses of the plains. It also has wild trefoils — herbs that produce hard and sour pastures. The ombu (*om*-boo) tree grows on the pampa, although it is slowly disappearing. It has wide-spreading leaves, a thick trunk, and roots that run along the ground.

Animal life in Argentina includes mountain lions, foxes, otters, deer, and the armadillo, a burrowing animal covered with bony plates. The pest of the pampa, and other agricultural areas, is the locust, a type of grasshopper that can strip the land of all its vegetation.

The pampa is a typical plains area. It is level and has few trees. The soil contains clay, silt, and fine sand. Once the pampa was a fertile wilderness. Now it is one of the most productive grasslands in the world.

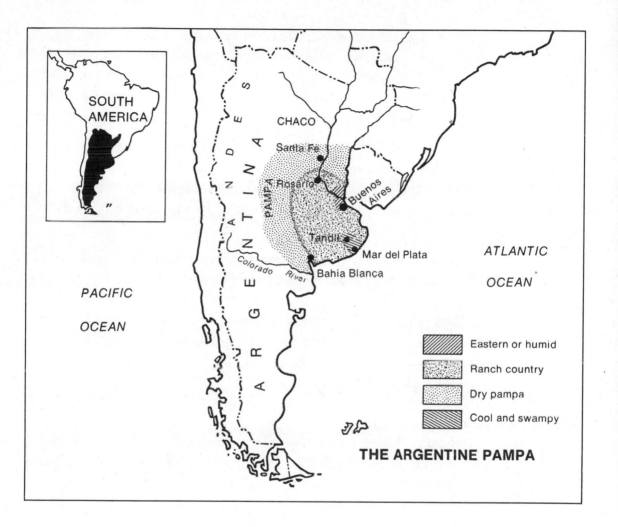

THE ARGENTINE PAMPA

Legend:
- Eastern or humid
- Ranch country
- Dry pampa
- Cool and swampy

The pampa can be divided into four regions:

An area around Buenos Aires, which supplies milk, fruit, and vegetables to the capital city. This eastern, or humid, pampa gets more rainfall than anywhere else on the great plain.

35

An area around Rosario, the country's second largest city. Cattle, maize, and flax are grown here. Cattle is one of the country's biggest industries, and the pampa is the heart of ranch country. Most of the cattle is raised in *estancias*, ranches which may cover thousands of acres.

The western belt, called the dry pampa. These 600 miles curve from Santa Fe in the north to Bahía Blanca in the south. This part of the pampa raises alfalfa, wheat, and some cattle. Wheat is the country's most important crop, and it is grown on almost one-fifth of all the farmland.

The cool and swampy southeastern region between Tandil and Mar del Plata. This area raises sheep and cattle.

When the Spaniards came to South America to colonize in the sixteenth century, the pampa was a vast plain covered with wild, tough grasses. In 1536, explorer Pedro de Mendoza founded a village on the site of what is now Buenos Aires. The name means "good air." By the end of the eighteenth century, the busy seaport had about 50,000 people living there.

Argentina became an independent country in 1816, after General José de San Martín (1778–1850) led the armies which drove Spain from the land.

But independence did not bring contentment to the new country. The next years were filled with civil war and rule by dictators. In 1853 the people of Argentina adopted a constitution that is very much like the Constitution of the United States.

The young country had many troubles during the late nineteenth century as it tried to grow in several ways. But despite their problems, the Argentinians managed to change the pampa from a wild plain into a productive grassland. The steel plow made it possible for farmers to

The flat and productive pampa

cut through the thick sod of the pampa. They planted alfalfa and more tender kinds of grass. By the end of the century Argentina led the world in the production of wheat and corn.

The cattle industry was well suited to the land of the pampa, and it grew larger and larger. In 1859 machinery was invented to drill wells on parts of the dry pampa. In 1873 barbed wire was invented to enclose ranches. These two inventions helped to make the cattle industry so successful.

The growing farms of Argentina suffered when Juan Perón became president in 1946. He wanted his country to become strong in industry. And so the farmers suffered. Many farms went out of business. By 1950 the whole country was suffering because of the farmers' troubles.

Perón was overthrown in 1955. Since then, leaders such as Juan

A town in the heart of the pampa

Gauchos at work

Carlos Ongania, who became president in 1966, have said that they would bring order back to their country.

The people of Argentina are independent and they are proud. This is especially true of the *gaucho*, the lonely rider of the pampa. He is a special type of person who feels that he is his own master.

The gaucho is the cowboy of Argentina and a hero to the people. He has been very important in the story of how the pampa was changed from wilderness to farmland. These hardworking cowboys are the backbone of Argentina's cattle industry.

The clothes of the gaucho make him stand out, too. His full, billowy trousers are called *bombachas*, and they are worn tucked into his leather boots. He wears a bright neckerchief and a colorful sash or leather belt, decorated with coins, around his waist. Today the gaucho is still an independent and proud man. But he may not roam over the pampa as he once did. He is just as likely to have settled down in a small town, or he may even be the owner of an estancia.

The Australian Lowlands

Australia is the smallest continent in the world. It is also the biggest island. Its nearly 3,000,000 square miles make it about the same size as the United States (excluding Alaska and Hawaii).

About one-third of the Commonwealth of Australia is grassland. The great interior plains, called the Central Lowlands, reach from the Gulf of Carpentaria in the north to Spencer Gulf in the south. They extend from the slopes of the Great Dividing Range in the east to western Queensland and to the Flinders Range in South Australia. The lowlands are generally less than 500 feet above sea level. There are also coastal plains around Perth, the state capital of Western Australia, and the treeless Nullarbor Plain in the south. Patches of high plains can be found in the eastern coastal highlands.

The Tropic of Capricorn divides Australia. One-third of the country is above it, and two-thirds below. The top one-third, which includes some plains land, is in the tropic zone. The lowlands, as might be expected, have unreliable rainfall. The average rainfall in the plains is from ten to twenty inches a year, but there are also periods of drought.

Few parts of Australia get enough rain. It is the driest of all the continents. That is one of the reasons why such a large land has so few people. Australia's population is below 15,000,000.

Rivers in the very northern plains area flow only in the summer. The southern section contains the all-important Murray River and its three branches, the Lachlan, the Darling, and the Murrumbidgee. The Darling is nearly 2,000 miles long, but it often runs dry during drought periods. The lowlands must depend upon artesian wells when water is scarce.

Even though so much of Australia is dry, the red-brown and black

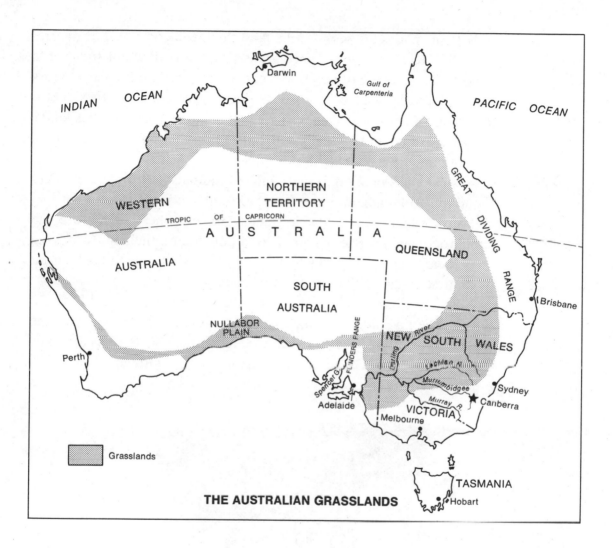

INDIAN OCEAN

PACIFIC OCEAN

Darwin

Gulf of Carpenteria

WESTERN

NORTHERN
TERRITORY

TROPIC OF CAPRICORN

A U S T R A L I A

AUSTRALIA

QUEENSLAND

GREAT DIVIDING RANGE

SOUTH

AUSTRALIA

Brisbane

NULLABOR
PLAIN

FLINDERS RANGE

NEW SOUTH WALES

Darling River

Perth

Spencer G.

Lachlan R.

Murrumbidgee

Adelaide

Murray R.

Sydney

Canberra

VICTORIA

Melbourne

Grasslands

TASMANIA

Hobart

THE AUSTRALIAN GRASSLANDS

soils of the plains are very fertile. And there is a good deal of natural plant life. Kangaroo grass once grew over the plains, but today it is almost gone because of sheep and cattle grazing. The kangaroo grass was replaced by wallaby and spear grasses, but much of these areas are gone, too. Australians have now planted grasses from other lands. They have also had to add phosphate fertilizers to the soil, since much Australian land is lacking in phosphates.

Australia has many different kinds of animals and birds. Some are found only on that continent. But the country is most famous for two creatures which live in the lowlands and elsewhere. They are the kangaroo, which carries its young in a pouch, and the cuddly-looking koala bear. The koala looks like a teddy bear. It seems to spend most of its time hugging the branches of eucalyptus trees.

Australia's birds include the emu, which can run very fast but cannot fly; the kookaburra, which has a strange laughing call; and the cassowary, whose speed has been clocked at nearly 40 miles an hour.

The rolling plains and gentle hills of the lowlands are Australia's greatest agricultural resource. This huge grassland grazes thousands

A koala bear caught napping

of sheep and cattle. There are thousands of square miles of good cattle country in Australia, most of it in the northern part.

Wool is Australia's biggest industry. The country produces about 30 percent of the world's wool. Australia is also one of the world's largest wheat producers. The wheat farms are found mainly in Victoria and New South Wales.

Dairy farms thrive in New South Wales and Queensland, and there are mixed farms throughout the lowland area. They grow oats, barley, maize, and wheat. These farms are much smaller than the sometimes huge cattle ranches, called stations, of the north.

The Dutch were the first Europeans to see Australia, which people had called *terra australis incognita,* or "unknown southern land." In the late eighteenth century, England began to send convicts there. The first colony, established in 1788 by the military and 726 convicts, was called Port Jackson. It later grew into what is now the city of Sydney.

In the early nineteenth century Captain John Macarthur began to breed Merino sheep in the good pastureland near Sydney. Merino sheep had flourished in the dry plains of Spain, and they soon began to flourish in the dry plains of Australia, too.

Convicts established other colonies in the land down under and explorers began to chart the continent. After the explorers came the sheepmen. They had been attracted by the promise of rich grazing lands, and Australia's plains did not disappoint them. These first sheepmen usually had no titles to the land. They just took over whatever they considered good pasture.

The six early colonies founded in this land grew into six states, and the Commonwealth of Australia was established on January 1, 1901. The federal capital is Canberra, in New South Wales. *Victoria* is the second smallest state in land area and second largest in population. Sheep and wheat are raised in the western lowland areas. Melbourne is the capital. *New South Wales* contains most of Australia's people. Its capital is Sydney, the largest city in the country. The western part of this state contains the nation's best grazing and wheat lands. There are also many mixed farms in New South Wales. *Queensland* is the nation's second largest state. The capital is Brisbane. Sheep and wheat are raised in the western lowlands. *Western Australia* is the largest of the states. Much of it is desert, although there are some sheep and wheat farms in the southwest. The capital is Perth. *South Australia*'s farms are in the southeast, but much of the state is too dry for agriculture. However, sheep graze on its natural grasslands. Adelaide is the capital city. The sixth state is *Tasmania,* an island south of Victoria. It is one of the few places in the country that has adequate rainfall. Hobart is the capital and largest city. The federally controlled *Northern Territory*, with its capital of Darwin, is the least populated area of Australia. It is too dry for farming, but some of its cattle stations cover over 1,000 square miles.

Rounding up cattle on the Australian plains

The Russian Steppe

The USSR is a nation of over 8,500,000 square miles. It is so large that it is separated, according to climate, into six different zones. At the far north is the Arctic tundra region. This joins the world's largest forest zone, covering almost half the area of the country. South of the forest zone is the forest steppe, where the trees begin to thin out. South of the forest steppe is the great Russian plain, covering about 964,000 square miles. And south of the plain are the desert and semidesert region and the subtropical zone.

The great plain of the USSR is known as the steppe. It is level, treeless, and grass-covered. This great farming area is generally less than 1,000 feet above sea level. The steppe makes up about two-thirds of Russia's farmland and about 12 percent of the country's total land area. It stretches from the western border of the USSR to the Yenisei River in Siberia, and from the Black Sea region north to the forest steppe. There are also scattered steppe regions in mountainous or semidesert spots.

The steppe climate is warm and the summers are dry. Rainfall is lowest in the southern part of the steppe; around the Caspian Sea the average is a little over six inches. Only a thin snow cover generally coats the ground in winter. However, winds from the southwest, called *sukhovey* (dry blower), often sweep across the land and cause much damage to the grain crop.

The southern steppe region bursts into bloom earlier than the northern part. Hyacinths may often bloom in the south as early as February. By mid-April the snow has melted in the north, and tulips and other flowers make their colorful appearances soon after. In June the steppe is a carpet of blue sage and feather grasses.

The natural cover of the steppe is shortgrasses. Little natural grass

The steppe

cover is left, however, since most of the steppe has been cultivated. Steppe grasses grow well in the fertile black soil. They include steppe fescue, pinnate feather grasses, and others.

Before this grassland was so highly cultivated, it was a playground for the roebuck, red deer, wild boar, and saiga antelope. Many birds, including the European partridge and the steppe eagle, live here. So do lizards, tortoises, and the common pest of the plains — the locust.

The black soil of the steppe is very fertile. In the north the soil is known as chernozem. It is deep, rich, and dark-colored. It may be from three to five feet thick. The soil in the drier southern steppe is a dark chestnut color. Around the Black Sea region are saucerlike holes in the land, called *pods*. They become temporary lakes when the snow melts. The soil here is porous and easily crumbled.

There are two reasons for the lack of trees in the steppe — the low rainfall and the poisonous salts beneath the lower layer of black soil.

The steppe is Russia's great breadbasket. But Soviet agriculture has been slowed by agricultural revolutions and a not always successful collective farm system. On the whole, progress in agriculture in the USSR has lagged behind progress in manufacturing or mining.

Nevertheless, the Russian steppe is a very productive agricultural land. Wheat is the leading crop. The steppe also produces corn, barley, oats, rye, potatoes, sugar beets, flax, and vegetable crops.

The first great agricultural change in the USSR came after the

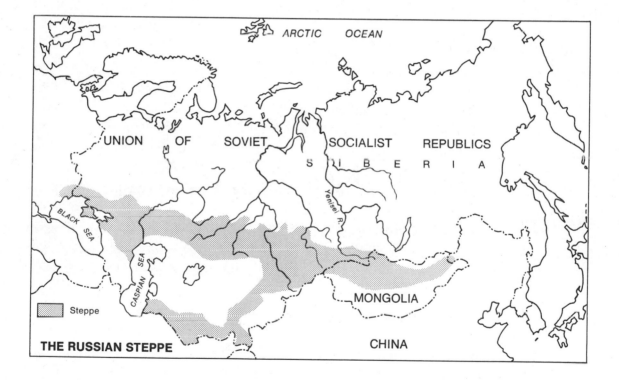

THE RUSSIAN STEPPE

revolutions of 1917. The first revolution, in March of that year, brought to an end the ruling house of Romanov. Czar Nicholas II (r. 1894–1917) was descended from the line which had produced such famous leaders as Peter I, known as Peter the Great (r. 1689–1725), and Catherine II, called Catherine the Great (r. 1762–96). The czar was toppled from his throne and later assassinated, along with his wife, son (the heir), and four daughters.

The country was now in the hands of liberal leaders. But the young and shaky government could not stop a second revolution, which occurred in November, 1917. It was called the Bolshevik Revolution for the party which came to power. The new head of state was Vladimir Ulyanov, better known as Lenin.

Lenin and his Bolshevik (the name was changed to Communist in 1918) party greatly altered the life of the Russian people. The Union of Soviet Socialist Republics (USSR) was formed in 1922. Old czarist Russia was now a Communist land.

Among the many changes which the Communists brought to the USSR was the revolution in agriculture. Private property was no more. The land was taken over by the peasants. The law said that land could not be bought or sold. The USSR became a country of many very small farms, worked by individual farmers.

Then, in 1929, the government began to promote the collective farm system. Lenin had died that same year, and the country was now ruled by Joseph Stalin.

Stalin introduced the five-year plans. These plans were intended to reach certain goals in agriculture during a five-year period. Stalin had not been pleased with the production of the individual steppe farmer. About 25 million small units were eventually grouped into some 240,000 collective farms. Stalin said that the larger farms would be easier to supervise and cheaper to run.

Trouble began almost immediately. Stalin had not counted on the stubbornness of the farmers. They wanted to work their own land instead of sharing in the profits from working on huge collective farms.

But the peasant farmer could not stand up against Stalin and the army. Many peasant farmers were killed and many others sent to labor camps. By 1934 the struggle was mainly over. The collective farms were established.

World War II brought great hardships to the USSR. The Germans overran much of its farmland. But at the war's end the collective farm system was set up once more.

Stalin introduced other five-year plans. So did Nikita Khrushchev, who became the country's leader in 1958. But after Stalin's death in 1953, the trend was toward fewer and bigger collective farms. By 1960 there were only about 44,000 of these farms in the USSR. The average size was 40,000 acres. Many state farms were set up, run by government-appointed managers. In the 1960's, a campaign was started to open up farmland in southern Siberia. It has been only partly successful, largely because of long droughts in the Siberian land.

Horses on the steppe

The Tundra of the North

The barren land of the Arctic is called the tundra. The name comes from a Finnish word that means "bare mountaintops." The tundra is very different from the plains and prairies in the rest of the world. It cannot be called a fertile grassland. Yet the tundra does have some things in common with all great plains. It is fairly level, with few trees, little rain, and a covering of grass, at least during the summer months.

The tundra belt runs along the coasts and islands of the Arctic Ocean, in Asia, Europe, and North America. In the USSR, the tundra covers 10 percent of the land. In all of the tundra, the climate and the plant and animal life are much the same.

The climate of the Arctic is anything but inviting. Winters are long and cold. In the heart of the tundra the monthly temperature may average 31 degrees below zero to an even 32 degrees, the freezing point of water. Summers are short and cool. No summer month (from late June to early September) averages higher than 50 degrees. The growing season is no longer than two and a half months.

Rainfall in the Arctic is only about eight to twelve inches a year, and much of the time strong winds sweep across the low, level land. Adding to the Arctic's dreariness is the lack of sunshine. As much as three-fourths of the sky is usually covered by clouds.

Except for some dwarf birches and willows scattered about, the tundra is treeless. In the summer months a kind of grass cover appears on the thawing topsoil. This shallow layer of topsoil lies over permanently frozen ground, known as the permafrost.

The Arctic's growing season is too short for annual plants to thrive and produce seeds. Instead, the ground is covered with mosses, which usually fill cracks in the rocks; lichens, which form crusts on the rock surfaces; and grasses and shrubs such as fescue and cowberry.

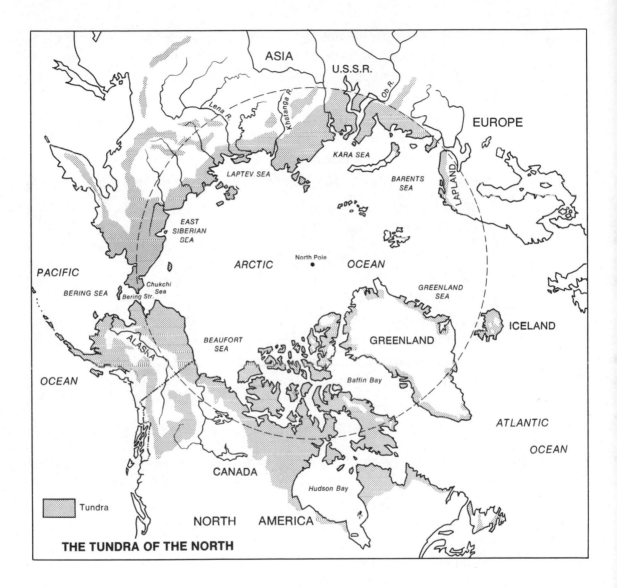

THE TUNDRA OF THE NORTH

ASIA

U.S.S.R.

EUROPE

Lena R.

Khatanga R.

Ob R.

KARA SEA

LAPTEV SEA

BARENTS
SEA

LAPLAND

EAST
SIBERIAN
SEA

PACIFIC

ARCTIC   North Pole   OCEAN

GREENLAND
SEA

Chukchi
Sea

BERING SEA

Bering Str.

ICELAND

OCEAN

ALASKA

BEAUFORT
SEA

GREENLAND

Baffin Bay

ATLANTIC

OCEAN

CANADA

Hudson Bay

Tundra

NORTH   AMERICA

This vegetation grows close to the ground as protection from the ever-blowing wind. In some spots during summer it is a surprise and a delight to see bright flowers — anemones, heather, buttercups — scattered over the land.

The northern tundra is often spoken of as three different regions:

The *Arctic tundra*, the land around the ocean, which has very little vegetation and few shrubs, lichens, and mosses.

The *shrubby tundra*, south of the Arctic tundra. It has some low willows and birches, and fescue and cowberry, as well as a few lichens, mosses, and peat bogs — masses of partly decomposed plants and mosses.

The *southern tundra*, which has many peat bogs, more scrubby birches and willows, and grasses, mosses, and lichens. (South of this region is the so-called *wooded tundra*, but it is not really part of the actual tundra. This is the area that meets forested land to the south, and it has thickets of scrub birches and willows.)

During the winter months the tundra is not an inviting place for human or animal life. One exception is the hardy polar bear. It visits the Arctic shores from its usual haunts on the pack ice. The polar bear has no challengers as king of the Arctic. It may grow ten feet in length and may weigh one thousand pounds.

Other animals that brave the tundra winter are the arctic fox, which is smaller than the regular fox, with a brown coat which turns white for protection in winter; the snowy owl; and the ptarmigan (*tar*-mi-gan), the state bird of Alaska. Its speckled brown coloring also turns white in winter.

In the summer the tundra comes to life with more animals. The wild reindeer come north for pastureland, and so do the wolves, which

There is sparse vegetation in the Arctic.

are fond of reindeer meat. The ratlike lemming leaves its underground home to search the tundra for food. These small animals have the strange habit of suddenly beginning to migrate across the tundra. They travel in one direction only and will try to cross anything in their path. Great numbers are lost — either drowned in lakes or the sea, or eaten by other animals along the route.

A rare but true creature of the tundra is the shaggy musk-ox. It looks something like the American bison. The musk-ox is protected from the cold Arctic temperatures by thick soft wool beneath its outer hair.

The tundra is also home to hare and caribou, and seals and walruses along the coasts. Many birds — such as Canadian geese, terns, ravens, and mergansers — invade the lakes in summer. Their shrill cries and flutterings bring color and noise to the dreary land of the North.

Musk-ox

There are no bats or snakes on the tundra, but there are mosquitoes — millions of them in summer. They are a great torment to animal and man alike.

There are not many recorded details of early history in the Arctic region. The Vikings explored around Iceland and Greenland in the late ninth century. Later, Eric the Red (father of Leif Ericson, who journeyed to the New World before Columbus) established a colony in Greenland.

About six hundred years later a great flurry of exploration invaded the Arctic. European adventurers began to search for a Northwest Passage. They were unsuccessful, but they charted much of the region in the process. The Dutchman Willem Barents, along with his crew, had the uncomfortable honor of being the first European to live through a winter in the frozen Arctic.

In the nineteenth century, man once again showed much interest in the land of the tundra, this time mainly for scientific reasons. And on April 6, 1909, Lieutenant Robert E. Peary of the United States Navy became the first man to stand at the North Pole.

Today the Arctic is still of great interest. The United States and the USSR, among other countries, are trying to develop the Arctic's natural resources — its mineral wealth in the permafrost. That wealth includes oil, gold, coal, iron, uranium, and other minerals.

The Arctic sits at the top of the world. That fact makes it important to many countries in a military way. For instance, the United States, with Canadian and European allies, has built a chain of radar stations across the Arctic. This defense network is called Distant Early Warning Line, or DEW Line. In August, 1958, as part of a military program, another "first" occurred in the Arctic. The nuclear-powered submarine U.S.S. *Nautilus* became the first ship to pass below the North Pole.

But the tundra of the north is still a forbidding place. Few people choose to call it home.

In North America the Arctic people include Eskimos, Aleuts, and Indians. There are probably about 60,000 Eskimos in the Arctic today. They are said to be part of the Mongoloid race. Their way of life has been greatly changed by the white settlers coming to the Arctic, especially to Alaska. It is surprising to most people to learn that the Eskimos generally have never seen a snowhouse, or igloo, much less lived in one. Except in the Canadian Arctic, most Eskimos live in homes of wood poles, caribou skins, and turf. However, any type of Eskimo home is known as an igloo, even though it is not made of snow blocks.

The Aleuts may have crossed over a land bridge from Siberia to Alaska thousands of years ago. Most of their small population lives today in the Aleutian Islands, the chain which stretches west from Alaska. The Indians of the tundra include the Little Whale River Indians and the Naskapi in northeastern Canada.

Probably the best-known people of the Arctic are the Laplanders, or Lapps. Without a country of their own, these small, sturdy people

A DEW Line station in Greenland

follow the reindeer herds across the tundra. Lapps still depend upon the reindeer, but today many of them have settled down in permanent homes, becoming fishermen and farmers. There are probably about 35,000 Laplanders in the Arctic, most of them in the region of Norway called Vidda.

The Arctic's largest population is in Siberia, in the Asiatic USSR. These people are divided into three main groups. The Altaics live generally around the Laptev Sea and in the Lena River basin. They used to be nomads in the Arctic, but today many are settling down on collective farms or to work in industry. The Paleo-Asiatic people either follow the reindeer as do the Lapps, or they hunt and fish on the Chukchi Peninsula across the Bering Strait from Alaska. The Uralian people are the largest of the Siberian tribes. Many live on the Arctic coast from the Khatanga River to the White Sea. Some are fishermen; others follow the reindeer herds.

Grasslands and Conservation

Man has learned how to build skyscrapers, to prevent polio, to fly to the moon. It is strange, indeed, that he has long seemed unable to learn how to conserve the natural resources of the planet upon which he lives. He pollutes clear water as though he could live without it; he hunts an animal to extinction as though he could re-create it; he ruins the land which gives him food as though he did not need to eat.

Grasslands, both in the United States and all over the world, have suffered from man's neglect of the land and his ignorance of conservation principles. When the United States was a very young country, it appeared to the new settlers that the varied and plentiful resources of the land would never end. They burned down forests without a thought to replanting; they dug up minerals without caring about wasting them; and they wore out the rich and fertile soil of many of the grassland areas by overgrazing and plowing.

Overgrazing can be a very slow process. The farmer may not even notice how thin the grass cover on his land has become — until weeds and scrubs take over and the land is dry and eroded. In some areas on the Great Plains, the land should never have been plowed at all. But farmers did not realize that in regions of fairly frequent drought, it is the grass which anchors the soil to the land. Remove the grass cover by plowing it under, and the dry soil is left to blow away by the tons. And so it did.

It is only in relatively recent years that much attention has been paid to conservation in the United States. However, as far back as 1877, Carl Schurz, secretary of the interior, recommended the establishment of federal forest reservations. Schurz, a former senator from Wisconsin, was born in Germany and had been trained in forestry practices there. The first forest reserve was set up in 1891.

57

Gifford Pinchot

Other men were interested in conservation, too. Major John Wesley Powell wrote about arid conditions in the West. He pointed out that the low rainfall in the area would not allow the traditional patterns of agriculture to succeed. The key word was water, and the success of farmers would depend upon irrigation. Powell wanted the Homestead Act to be revised so that the amount of land to be farmed was based upon the available water. But he watched helplessly as cattle overgrazed the land of the Great Plains, and nothing was done to conserve the fertile grasslands.

Gifford Pinchot, made chief of the Forest Service in 1898, was also intensely interested in conservation. He urged a program for the management of the country's forests.

In 1934 the Taylor Grazing Act was passed. It closed public domain lands to homesteading and it set up a program to prevent erosion and to control overgrazing. The following year the Soil Erosion Service was started. Its purpose was to stop or to control soil erosion.

Gradually, it is being realized in the United States, and all over the world, that conservation practices must be followed if grasslands, forests, and water supply are to be healthy and productive.

Some of the methods used to preserve the grasslands include crop rotation, cover crops, terracing, and strip-cropping. Crop rotation means alternating the planting of various crops. Growing such things as soybeans and clovers returns nitrogen to the soil, a necessary mineral for healthy land production. Cover crops may be planted to enrich and protect the soil. If the land is left uncovered, it becomes the victim of erosion. On hills or sloping fields, terracing — a series of broad ridges of earth — has been successful. Strip-cropping — planting alternate strips of close-growing and other crops — is a popular conservation method in Europe.

Strip-cropping

In some areas of the world, grasslands have been ruined to the extent that only long years of careful conservation practices will bring them back to productive use. In other places, knowledge and understanding by dedicated farmers and conservationists have kept the grasslands healthy and fertile. As the world's population increases, so does the problem of feeding people. A key to solving that problem is the preservation of one of the earth's most precious natural resources — the grasslands.

Where to See Our National Grasslands

The map on the following page shows the names and locations of national grasslands in the United States. These areas were bought by the government in the drought-ridden 1930's. They became a part of the National Forest System and are administered by the U.S. Forest Service. The plan was to make these lands, which were almost useless because of bad conservation practices, natural grasslands once again. As part of the project, grass is grown in these areas and the growth of native animal life is encouraged.

Outside of the national grasslands, it is still possible to see some natural grassland areas in eastern Kansas and Montana, in western Iowa, in central Nebraska, and in patches of Wisconsin and Minnesota, as well as in the western states of California, Washington, and Oregon.

NATIONAL GRASSLANDS

WASHINGTON

CROOKED RIVER
OREGON

MONTANA

LITTLE MISSOURI
NORTH DAKOTA

MINN.

CEDAR RIVER
GRAND RIVER

SHEYENNE

SOUTH DAKOTA
FORT PIERRE

THUNDER BASIN
WYOMING

BUFFALO GAP

WISCONSIN

MICHIGAN

NEW YORK

MAINE

VT. N.H.

MASS.

R.I.
CONN.

PENN.

N.J.

IDAHO

NEBRASKA

IOWA

ILLINOIS

INDIANA

OHIO

W. VA.

DEL.
MD.

NEVADA

UTAH

PAWNEE
COLORADO

KANSAS

MISSOURI

KENTUCKY

VIRGINIA

NORTH CAROLINA

CALIFORNIA

COMANCHE
CIMARRON

TENNESSEE

SOUTH CAROLINA

ARIZONA

KIOWA
RITA BLANCA

BLACK KETTLE

NEW MEXICO

OKLAHOMA

ARKANSAS

MISSISSIPPI

ALABAMA

GEORGIA

LAKE MC CLELLAN

CROSS TIMBERS
TEXAS

LOUISIANA

FLORIDA

National Grasslands

A Glossary of Grassland Words

BAMBOO — tall, fast-growing grasses

CEREAL GRASSES — grains with seeds that can be eaten, such as rice and corn

COVER CROPS — crops which are planted to enrich and protect the soil

CROP ROTATION — alternating the planting of various crops, a conservation method

EROSION — wearing away of the land by water, heat, wind, etc.

GAUCHO — cowboy of the Argentine pampa

GRASSES — largest of all the plant families

GRASSLAND — area with a natural cover of grass instead of trees

LEA — grassy place to graze animals

LOWLANDS — plains area, such as in Australia

MEADOW — grassy, often moist, place to graze animals

PAMPA — the great plain of Argentina

PASTURE — *see* Lea

PASTURE GRASS — grass on plains and prairies good for grazing cattle

PLAIN — large, mostly level area of land

PRAIRIE — treeless area with a natural cover of tallgrasses

SAVANNA — plain in a warm climate

SHORTGRASS — natural cover of plains

STATIONS — cattle ranches in Australia

STEPPE — plain in Europe and Asia

STRIP-CROPPING — planting alternate strips of close-growing and other crops, a conservation method

SWEET GRASS — grass with a sweet juice, such as sugarcane

TALLGRASS — natural covering of prairies

TERRACING — series of broad ridges of earth, a conservation method

TREFOILS — herbs that produce hard and sour pastures
TUNDRA — level, treeless plain in the Arctic
VELD — grassland in Africa

A Selected Bibliography

Archer, Sellers G., and Clarence E. Bunch. *The American Grass Book*. Norman: University of Oklahoma Press, 1953.

Berg, Lev S. *Natural Regions of the U.S.S.R*. New York: Macmillan, 1950.

Cairns, G. O. and J. F. *Australia*. London: Black, 1955.

Cole, Monica M. *South Africa*. London: Methune, 1961.

Costello, David F. *The Prairie World*. New York: Crowell, 1969.

Donahue, Roy L., Everett F. Evans, and L. I. Jones. *The Range and Pasture Book*. Englewood: Prentice-Hall, 1956.

Greenwood, Gordon. *Australia*. New York: Praeger, 1955.

Hance, William A. *The Geography of Modern Africa*. New York: Columbia.

Heintzelman, Oliver H., and Richard M. Highsmith, Jr. *World Regional Geography*. Englewood: Prentice-Hall, 1955.

Kraenzel, Carl Frederick. *The Great Plains in Transition*. Norman: University of Oklahoma Press, 1955.

Malin, James C. *The Grassland of North America*. Kansas: self-published, 1961.

Mirov, N. T. *Geography of Russia*. New York: Wiley, 1951.

Oliver, Roland, and J. D. Fage, *A Short History of Africa*. New York University Press, 1964.

Pendle, George. *Argentina*. London: Oxford University Press, 1961.

Shabad, Theodore. *Geography of the U.S.S.R*. New York: Macmillan, 1950.

Staten, H. W. *Grasses and Grassland Farming*. New York: Devin-Adair, 1952.

Thompson, Henry D. *Fundamentals of Earth Science*. New York: Appleton-Century-Crofts, 1960.

Udall, Stewart L. *The Quiet Crisis*. New York: Holt, Rinehart and Winston, 1963.

Webb, Walter Prescott. *The Great Plains*. New York: Ginn, 1931.

Index

Musk-ox, 53

National Forest Systems, 60
Nautilus, U.S.S., 55
Needlegrasses. *See* Prairie, U. S., grasses.

Oats. *See* Cereal grasses.
Overgrazing, 17, 57

Pampa, 4, 28, 33-39
   animals, 34, 36
   climate, 34, 35
   grasses, 34
   history, 36, 38
   location, 34
   soil, 34
Pastures, 3
Pasture grasses, 1, 2, 12
Pinchot, Gifford, 58
Plains, 2, 4, 8
   See also Great Plains, Lowlands, Steppe, Veld.
Plow, invention of, 24, 36, 38
Polar bear, 52
Powell, John Wesley, 58
Prairie dogs, 13, 14
Prairies, 1, 2, 19-28
Prairie, U. S., 19-28
   animals, 22, 23
   birds, 22
   climate, 20, 21
   grasses, 21
   location, 19
   plants, 21, 22
Pronghorn antelope, 13

Rabbits, 14
Rice. *See* Cereal grasses.
Rye. *See* Cereal grasses.

Savannas, 4, 8, 29
Schurz, Carl, 57
Sheep industry, 9, 17, 31, 42-44

Shortgrasses, 4, 11, 12
Siberia, people in, 56
Side oats grama. *See* Great Plains, grasses.
Sodbusters, 24
Soil Erosion Service, 58
South Africa. *See* Veld.
Steppe, 4, 45-49
   animals, 46
   birds, 46
   climate, 45
   grasses, 45, 46
   history, 48, 49
   location, 45
   plants, 45
   soil, 46
Strip-cropping, 59
Sugarcane. *See* Sweet grasses.
Sweet grasses, 1, 2
Switch grass. *See* Prairie, U. S., grasses.

Tall grasses, 1, 19, 21
Taylor Grazing Act, 58
Terracing, 59
Tundra, 4, 50-56
   animals, 52, 53
   birds, 53
   climate, 50
   grasses, 50, 52
   history, 54-56
   location, 50

U.S.S.R. *See* Steppe.

Veld, 4, 28, 29-33
   animals, 31
   climate, 30, 31
   history, 32, 33
   soil, 31

Western wheatgrass. *See* Great Plains, grasses.
Wheat. *See* Cereal grasses.